Milton ... Primary PRU
"Our Library of Imagination -
A Place of 1000 Amazing Adventures"

SNAP!

BY JENNY OLDFIELD

LDA

SNAP!

Snap!
LL00756
ISBN 1 85503 189 2
© Jenny Oldfield
© cover design and illustrations Ted Lazlo Design
All rights reserved
First published 1993
Reprinted 1994, 1996, 1999, 2001, 2002

Printed in the UK for LDA
LDA, Duke Street, Wisbech, Cambs, PE13 2AE, UK
3195 Wilson Dr. NW, Grand Rapids, MI 49544, USA

1

Snap!

Some kids like books. Some kids like sport. But Molly liked cameras.

She did not like her name, or her two big front teeth. She did not like her big brother, Paul. But she did like cameras.

Her dad gave her one when she was 10. 'Keep it safe,' he said. 'Cameras are fun, but they soon break. You must take care!'

Molly knew that. She kept the camera in its black case. It sat in its case, black and silver and shiny. She rubbed the lens until it shone. The lens winked back at her like an eye.

'Hm,' Molly's mum said when she showed her the camera. 'Trust your dad to spoil you!' Mrs Spence did not smile. She told Molly to sit in the car. Molly waited for her mum to talk to her dad, then they drove home.

'Dad says he'll teach me to print photos!' Molly said. 'In his dark room.'

Mrs Spence said nothing.

'I always wanted a camera!' Molly said.

Still Mrs Spence said nothing.

'And now I've got one!' Molly did not care what her mum thought. She was over the moon.

⋄

Next day it was fine, just right for taking photos.

Molly could take twenty-four photos with the film. She knew how to point the camera. She knew which buttons to press.

'Mum, I'm going out to take some photos!' she yelled. Her mum was washing up.

'Who with?'

'Susie!'

'Susie Martin?' her mum checked.

'Yes!'

'Be back in half an hour!' Her mum wanted to go to the shops.

'OK!' Before Mrs Spence changed her mind, Molly shot off.

'And mind you don't lose that camera!' her mum called.

Snap!

'As if!' Molly said to herself. Susie and she ran into the park. The ducks stood on the cold ice and quacked. The frost made the trees stiff and white.

'Take a photo of the ducks!' Susie said. 'Quick!'

Molly snapped the poor ducks. She snapped the frost in the trees. Then she snapped Susie hanging from a frozen branch. Her hair touched the ground.

They ran on past Molly's brother, Paul, and Dean Smith. Paul did not say hello. They ran over the old bridge.

'Take a photo of the church!' Susie told her.

Molly looked through the camera lens, but the church was too big. Only the door would fit in the photo. 'I can't fit it all in,' she said.

'Never mind. Take it!'

Molly pressed the button just as a man came out of the wide door. Click! The man was dressed in a long, dark coat. He had a big grey scarf round his face. He carried a black bag. 'Hey!' he shouted when he saw Molly's camera. He came up and tried to grab it.

But Molly was quick. She saw the look in his eyes and she ran away holding her

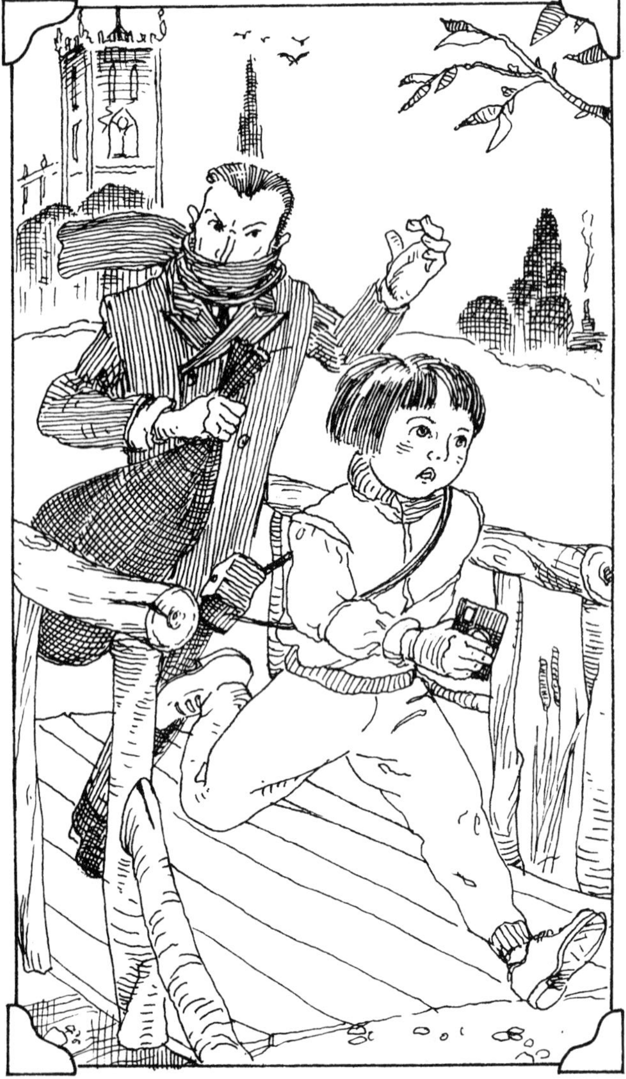

camera tightly.

The man ran over the bridge after her. She heard his steps, she felt his breath. He chased her into the frosty white park.

'Watch it!' Paul said. Some man was chasing his sister. Dean and Paul stuck out their legs to trip the man. He fell. He and his bag crashed to the ground. But Molly was safe!

The four of them, Dean, Paul, Susie and Molly, ran straight past the swings up the hill. The man stood up, covered in frost, and stared after them.

They stopped running at the park gates. 'Am I glad to see you!' Molly said to Paul. She never thought she would say that to her own brother!

2

The Empty Church

Molly sat and ate her toast.

'I don't want you to wander off!' her mum said again. 'You hear me, Molly!' Mrs Spence poured the orange juice. 'Just because your dad's given you that camera, it doesn't mean you can wander off!'

Molly nodded. She wished she had not told her mum about the man in the park. She ate her toast and read the newspaper.

'Your fringe needs cutting!' Mrs Spence said. She always found something to nag about. 'Come here! Stand still!'

Molly watched her dark hair fall on to the newspaper. Snip, snip. Pieces of fringe fell on to the paper. On it there was a picture of a church and big black words above it, THIEF STEALS STATUES FROM CHURCH!

The Empty Church

Molly jumped.

'Stand still!' her mum said. She held the scissors up in the air.

'Mum!' Molly pointed at the picture of the church. 'Mum!'

'What is it, Molly?'

'The church! The man in the park!'
'It was him! It was the man who stole the statues!'

'Don't be silly!' Mrs Spence looked at the newspaper. She looked at Molly jumping up and down. 'Are you sure?'

'Yes, I'm sure! He came out of the church door with a big heavy bag. He saw me take his picture! He chased me and Susie. He did!' Molly grabbed the newspaper. Bits of her fringe fell on the floor.

'Molly!' Mrs Spence moaned. She went for a brush to sweep it up.

Molly read the words under the picture:

A brass plate and two small stone statues were stolen from All Saints' Church, Mirton, on Wednesday 2nd January. Police say that the statues are at least six hundred years old. They describe them as very valuable.

'What does "valuable" mean?'

'Worth a lot of money,' Paul said. He piled jam on his toast. He yawned.

'How much?'

'I don't know. It doesn't say.'

'But I saw him!' Molly said again. Why did they not believe her?

Paul shrugged. 'So?'

'I could go and tell the police!' she said.

'You stay out of this, Molly!' her mum warned. She swept the floor and shook her head. 'I knew this camera meant trouble.' She stood up. 'Now listen, Molly, if I hear any more nonsense because of this silly camera, I'll take it away, do you hear?'

Molly nodded. Her mum meant what she said. She did not want to lose her camera. 'OK,' she said.

✧

But she and Susie went down to the church anyway.

They stopped at the swings in the park. The frost had melted, and it was misty and damp.

'We could just go and look,' Molly said. 'It's only just over the bridge.'

The Empty Church

'What harm is there?' Susie said.

So they walked along the river bank, over the stone bridge. They tried to look as if they were just going for a walk up the church path.

'Ssh!' Molly said. She led the way.

They opened the big wooden door. It creaked. Inside it was very dark. The church smelled of damp plaster. White flakes of paint were falling off the wall. Molly and Susie walked towards the cross.

'What are we looking for?' Susie whispered. You had to whisper in a church.

'Clues!' Molly said.

But she did not really know. She looked at the carved wooden seats, the big metal organ pipes. There were two stone people lying on their backs, lying on a flat table. There was a carved eagle. There was a big Bible open, ready to read from.

'Look!' Molly said suddenly.

She pointed to a place on the floor. It was a mess. The stone was chipped and there was a pale square hollow. The brass plate had gone from there. 'And look!' Molly said again. She pointed to two gaps in a row of statues above the altar.

Susie stared. 'But where are the clues?' she said.

Molly sighed. They just stood there in front of the altar, trying to think.

'Hey!' A man came out of the little door beside the organ pipes. 'Hey, you two!'

Was it him again? Was it the thief? Molly grabbed Susie's hand and ran. They did not stop to look. They ran out of the church through the huge door.

They stopped for breath on the old bridge. Molly leant against the low wall.

'Was it him?' Susie wanted to know. 'Was it the same man?'

Molly shook her head. Her throat was sore, her lungs hurt. 'I don't know!' she looked back, but there was no one following. 'I wish I'd brought my camera!' she gasped.

3

Stop Thief!

Molly took her camera to her dad's house. Her mum dropped her at the door as usual.

'Have you used up your film?' her dad asked. He showed her how to wind it to the end and take it out of the camera. 'Have you got some good shots?'

They went into the attic. 'Darkroom' it said on the door, and below, 'Do Not Disturb'.

The room was full of tables and shelves. There were bottles, trays, a sink and things for washing, drying and cutting the film. Her dad had a special light bulb in the darkroom. It made his face glow red.

Molly loved the sharp smell in the dark room. She loved to watch her dad hang up the negatives to dry. Then they looked at each square on the strip. Everything was the wrong way round. Susie's fair hair

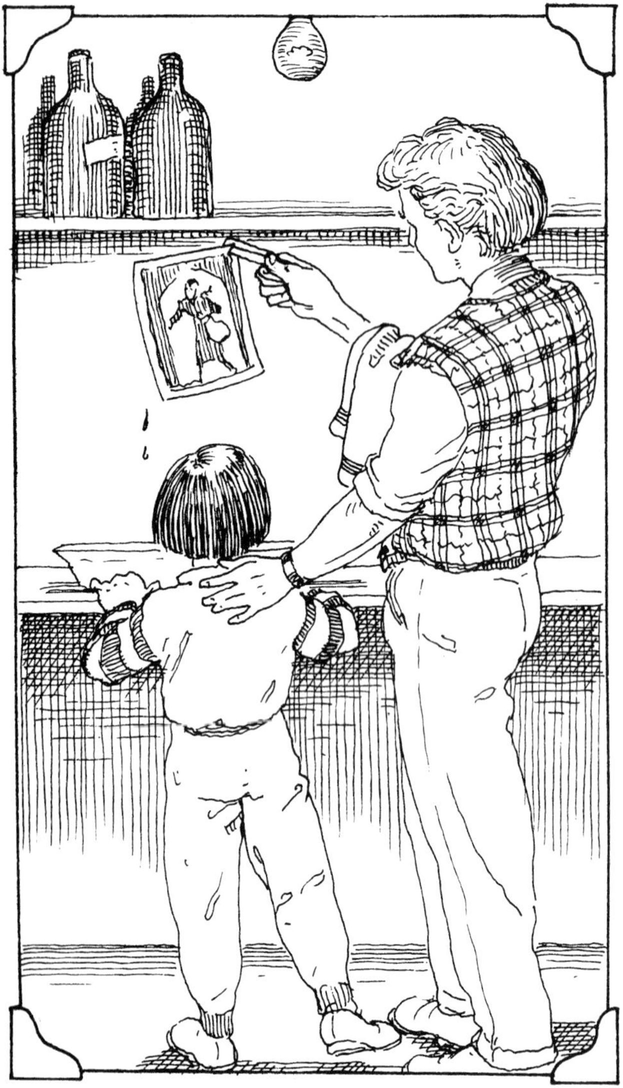

Stop Thief!

was black. Molly's dark hair was white.

'Let's print them!' her dad said.

Molly watched. There were the ducks on the ice. There was Susie hanging from the tree. She came up slowly on the white paper. Mr Spence swished the paper in the tray. Shadows appeared, the branch of a tree, Susie's face. Then they washed the photos in the sink.

'Let's try another,' Mr Spence said.

On the next square of paper the church door appeared first. Then a ghostly shadow. Molly held her breath. 'It's him!' she whispered. The shadow turned into the thief like magic. She saw his long, dark coat and his scarf. The photograph was printed. It was a picture of the thief!

Molly washed it and hung it up to dry. It was clear and sharp.

'Good photo,' her dad said. He looked at the man in the church doorway.

'It's a clue!' Molly told him, smiling.

Even the thought of school on Monday could not spoil Molly's good mood.

She took the picture of the thief along to show Susie. 'I printed it myself,' Molly told her. They sat on the bench outside Woolworth's. Molly met up with Susie every

SNAP!

Saturday at 11.

'What do we do now?' Susie asked.

'I don't know. Do you know who he is?' Molly said. 'Have you ever seen him before?' She had already asked Paul and Dean. They had said no.

'Haven't a clue,' Susie said.

They went round town asking all their friends, 'Do you know this man?' Everyone said no. They ended up back at Woolworth's.

'What now?' Susie said, sighing. It was fun trying to find clues, trying to catch a thief, but she was hungry.

She looked at her watch. 'I'd better go,' she told Molly. 'We'll make plans later.'

And off she went. Molly was not hungry. She kept trying to find someone who knew the man in the photo.

She stood outside Boot's talking to Dean and his mates.

'Yeh, yeh,' Dean said. She handed the picture round the gang, 'You're an ace detective, Molly Spence!' He sounded fed up. But then Dean always sounded fed up, like Paul. The other kids said no, they had never seen the man before.

'Good photo though, Molly,' Stacey

14

Stop Thief!

Jones said kindly. She handed it back.

Then there was a push and the photo went flying. Molly tried to grab it as a man pushed his way into the middle of the gang. *The* man! Tall, dark, angry.

The photo fell to the ground. Dean tried to stamp on it with his boot. But the man was quicker. He snatched it from the ground.

'Stop!' Molly shouted.

The man pushed her back against Stacey. All the gang pushed and shoved. Arms and legs were all over the place. Little Molly was lost in the middle of it. 'Stop him!' she yelled. Someone grabbed her jacket. 'Get the photo! Stop him!'

But the shoppers in the street just stood and stared. The man ran off, still holding the photo.

'It's only a snapshot,' Stacey said, trying to fix her hair. 'What's all the fuss?'

Molly did not stop to explain. She saw the man take off down a side alley. She followed him. This time she had her camera. She ran into the car park after the thief.

She saw him jump into a big white van. She got her camera ready.

The van started up.

15

She lifted her camera. There was a side view of the van. Click! Click! Click! Three shots. The white van shot off out of the car park. She read the sign on the side of the van. 'Manor House Antiques' it said, in gold and red letters.

4

Manor House Antiques

This time Molly did not even wait to finish the film. Instead she wound it to the end, took it out of the camera and put it in an envelope. She wrote a note:

Dear Dad,
Please print what's on this film. It's very important. It's a clue to a robbery. Please hurry.
Love from

Molly
xxx

Paul said he would take it for her. He was going over to their dad's that afternoon.

'Food time!' Mrs Spence said from the kitchen.

Molly went down and gobbled her burger and chips.

'What's the rush?' Paul asked. He had his feet up, watching sport on the TV.

Molly did not have time to explain. 'I'm going to town,' she told her mum.

'Again?' Mrs Spence cleared the table. 'Don't be long!' she shouted.

Molly went to the library. 'Excuse me, I'm looking for a list of antique shops in Mirton,' she told the lady at the desk.

The woman looked down at a small, dark-haired child with a short fringe. 'Pardon?'

'I need to find an antique shop called Manor House Antiques,' Molly said in a rush.

'Oh, I know where that is!' the lady said with a smile. 'It's across town, next to the museum. You know, just before the road up to the moor.' She took off her glasses for a better view of Molly. 'Why?'

'Never mind. Thanks!' Molly hopped from one foot to the other. 'I'd best be off!'

'I say!' The woman called her back. 'You forgot something!' She held up Molly's camera.

Molly went red. She went back for the camera. 'Thanks.'

She was soon out on the street. She

Manor House Antiques

knew the museum by the moor. It was a place full of old paintings and maps of Mirton. Her mum dragged her in there sometimes. She found it easily.

On one side of the museum was a cafe. On the other side the sign above a shop said 'Manor House Antiques' in red and gold letters.

Molly felt a little jump in her tummy. This was how it felt to solve a mystery. Exciting, but a bit scary. The antique shop was in an old stone house with narrow windows. There was a dim light inside. Molly crept towards it.

The window was full of shelves. They were loaded with glass and silver objects, gold chains and china birds. Molly pretended to look at them. What next? She tried to peep inside. There was someone there!

Suddenly Molly lost her nerve. She darted next door into the museum. Her legs had gone weak.

'Hey, who's with you?' the man at the desk barked. He looked like a bulldog with his flat nose and droopy eyes.

'No one,' Molly gasped.

'Then hop it!' the man snarled.

'What?'

'Hop it, go on! No children without adults, see!' He pointed to a notice. 'Can't you read!'

'I'm sorry,' Molly said weakly. 'I just thought....'

But the man at the desk did not want her to think. She backed out into the cold, misty afternoon.

'Right,' she said to herself, 'this time I'm going in!' She went to the antique shop and went in.

'Can I help you?' a woman asked.

Molly tried to get used to the dark room. It was full of big wooden chests, chairs, fancy plates. It smelt of polish. An old black sheepdog slept flat out by a fan heater.

'Yes, please?' the woman said.

'I want – er – a very old camera!' Molly said on the spur of the moment. It was all she could think of. She saw that the woman was neat and white haired, with a pearl necklace. She relaxed and looked round more carefully.

'Wait a moment.' The old woman poked about behind the counter. Then she went through a door at the back of the shop.

Molly saw a box of old medals. There

Manor House Antiques

were old brown books on shelves and painted plates on the wall. There was even a stuffed fox in a glass case. But no stone statues, no brass plate. She jumped as the old lady came back.

'No, I'm afraid we don't have any old cameras at the moment.' She looked at Molly. 'Mr Woodhouse says we sometimes get the old Brownie cameras. But not just at the moment.'

Molly nodded. 'Thanks,' she said. This place was making her heart beat faster. She longed to be out in the fresh air.

'Try again!' the old lady said.

Molly opened the door. Outside it was already growing dark. She took a deep breath.

But she was not put off, not now she had got this far. She took her camera out of its soft case. She pressed a button, heard the whine of the battery in the flash unit. At last a tiny red light came on. She held up the camera and took a shot of the front of the shop. The flash lit up the courtyard.

The man from the museum came to the door. The old lady from Manor House Antiques came to the window.

So Molly moved off, but not far. She

tiptoed round the back of the museum.

The street light glowed orange. Night had fallen. Molly crept along the grass at the back of the museum. She peeped over a wall. Her heart went thud. There in the yard was the white van. Its back doors were open. She lifted her camera. Ready to take more pictures.

5

The Chase

But Molly heard a noise. She ducked behind some dustbins. The back door of the museum opened and the bulldog man from the desk came out in his brown uniform. He looked to the left and the right.

Molly held her breath. She hugged her camera tight. The museum man walked across the yard. His jacket brushed against the dustbins, but he did not see Molly. He opened a gate and went into the yard where the white van was parked. Molly dared to take another peek.

Someone jumped down from the van. It was dark, but Molly knew who it was. He was tall and thin, very mean looking. It was the thief!

He stood face to face with the museum man. Bulldog said something angry and pointed to the museum. Thief snapped

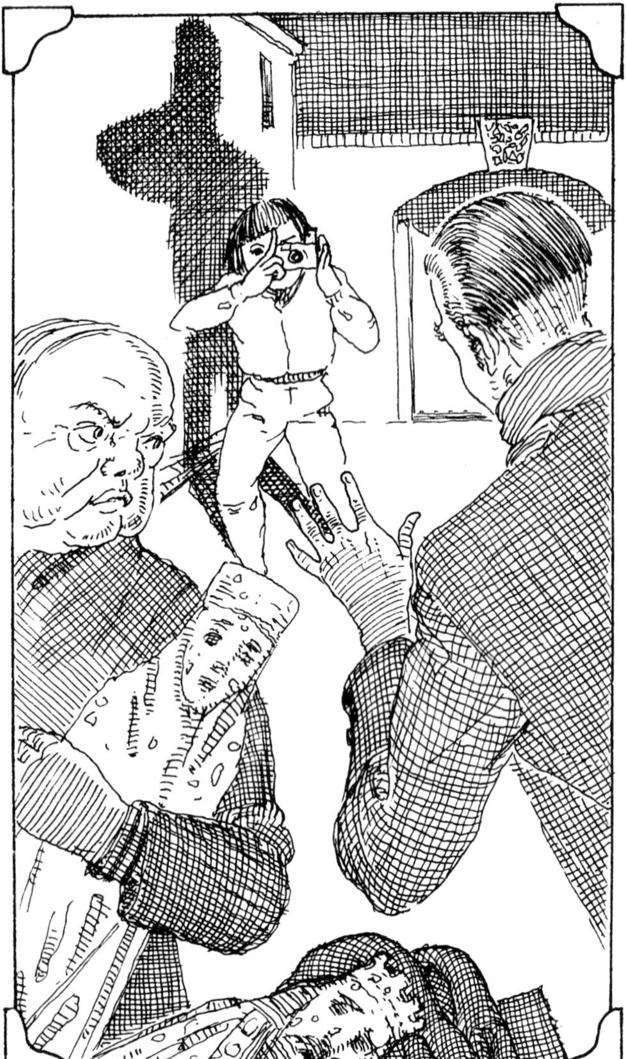

The Chase

back, shook his head. 'Look,' he said. He pulled a small square of white paper out of his pocket and tore it in two. He was laughing now. Molly saw Bulldog nod. He grunted. 'Come on, let's get a move on.'

They got inside the van. A few seconds passed. Bulldog backed out first with something heavy. Then the thief came out, with another load. The statues! Molly nearly jumped up and gave herself away. They stood in the yard behind the antique shop, holding the stolen statues.

Molly thought fast. Here was the proof she needed. Take a photo, plan an escape, run off as fast as she could. It was a big risk. Dare she do it? Her hands shook as she pressed the button on her camera to charge up the flash. She was cold, her fingers were stiff. The men began to move off.

At the last moment she stood straight up, aimed the camera, and flash! She got them!

The men got the shock of their lives. Molly had got them on film.

She did not hang around. She jumped over the dustbins, dashed for the road. A gate banged. The men were chasing her.

Molly reached the road. She did not

have time to think. She ran up towards the moor, her camera in one hand. She could run fast. She would lose them up on the moor.

She could hear them breathing hard. They were still following. Her own lungs hurt. She ran up the hill into the damp, dark night.

The thief could run fast too. He was catching her up. She must try to hide. She jumped through the heather. It scratched her legs and pulled her down. She picked herself up. She was gasping for breath.

The man sounded very near now. She looked back. His shadowy shape was very close. Molly made one last effort and threw herself behind a huge black rock. She lay flat on the ground and held her breath.

Had he seen her? He crashed on through the heather. He stopped. He jumped up on to *her* rock to look around. The bulldog man caught up, panting for breath. 'She's round here somewhere,' the thief told him.

'Hiding?' The fat man crouched down, ready to search.

The thief nodded. He got out a torch and switched it on. The two of them started kicking the bushes, swiping at the ferns and looking behind all the rocks. Molly bit her lip and lay still as a stolen statue.

The torch beam moved away, then came back towards her. It flicked over her rock! She must move. She must try to get away. They would find her next time for sure. She began to back away on all fours. One sound would finish her!

'Ssh!' the thief said. They stood and listened. When the torch beam swung away from her again, Molly stood and made a dash. She ran like the wind. The ground was clear. She ran until her lungs gave out.

Suddenly she was right up against a stone wall! A straight, smooth, towering cliff face. There was no way up, no way around. It was Mirton Rock. She had run into a dead end!

Molly turned. The men stood and faced her. In the torch beam her face was like a pale, scared rabbit's. Her eyes stared wide.

The thief came right up to her. He grabbed her camera. He pulled it away. He grinned as he swung it by its strap.

Then he smashed it straight against the black rock. It broke into a dozen pieces.

It was as if something broke inside Molly too. Her camera glinted in the torchlight, broken into pieces. The thief put his foot on it hard. The bits of her camera were crushed into the ground.

6

Alone in the Dark

They took her, kicking and struggling, back down the moor into town. It was a dark, misty night with no one around. Bulldog had his hand over Molly's mouth so she could not scream.

The shops were closed. The cafe next to the museum was all shut up.

'Right,' the museum man said. 'What now?'

They stood next to the white van in the antique shop yard. Molly shook like a leaf.

'This kid knows all about us. What are we going to do about it, Woodhouse?'

If looks could kill, Molly would have been dead on the floor. Woodhouse, the thief, stared meanly at her. Then he curled his lip. 'She's only a kid,' he sneered. 'Who'd believe a kid?'

The other man blew clouds of steam into the night air. 'Stupid kid!' he muttered.

Molly knew when to stay quiet.

'Listen, I've already got the first photo back off her, haven't I?' Woodhouse said. 'The one of me at the church. And the stupid camera is buried in the dirt up at Mirton Rock!' He grinned.

'I still don't want her messing things up for us!' the fat man said. 'We've got to do something about this kid!' He pointed a stubby finger at Molly.

Woodhouse nodded. He shoved Molly towards the back door of the shop. 'After you!' he sneered. Molly fell forward.

She half-fell into a dim, dark room. She knocked her shin against something and bent forward in pain. 'Turn the light on,' Woodhouse said. 'Let the young lady see where she's going!'

In the yellow light Molly saw what it was she had fallen over. The small statue from the church! And another, and another and another! Big and small, standing, lying, leaning, there were loads of them. All stolen, she thought, grey and worn, like ghosts from the past.

Woodhouse watched her mouth fall open in surprise. He laughed. 'We steal them, then ship them out,' he said. 'To Japan, the Middle East, anywhere we can

Alone in the Dark

sell them! We make a fortune!'

Molly thought of all the poor robbed churches, but Woodhouse pushed her out of the way. 'We'll get rid of these tonight,' he said to the other man, 'instead of tomorrow. It makes no difference.' And the two of them began to load the statues into the van. 'Sit tight, don't move!' he snapped at Molly.

She sat on the cold floor hugging her knees. She tried not to cry. What would they do to her once they had moved the statues into the van?

The work seemed to take ages. To and from the van they went, staggering under the weight of some of the bigger statues. At last Woodhouse slammed the back doors of the van shut. 'Get in!' he told the museum man. Then he came back.

Molly looked up at him. 'My mum will come looking for me!' she tried to warn him. But her voice did not sound brave.

He laughed. 'Where will she look, then?' He checked the window to see if it was locked. He checked another door. 'Just to make sure,' he said. Then he took a piece of blue rope, the sort you use to tow a car. 'Hold out your hands!' He tied up her arms

31

and feet, then sat her down in an old leather chair. 'Carter's right, we can't be too careful,' he said.

'My brother will be looking too!' Molly said. She choked back tears. 'And my dad!'

But Woodhouse took no notice. His footsteps rang out on the stone floor. He stopped at the door and turned out the light.

Molly was left in darkness. She heard the key turn in the lock. She heard the van engine roar and move off. It was pitch black inside the room.

There was one thing she dreaded and this was it. She did not mind spiders and she did not mind heights. She did not mind the Superlooper at the theme park. But she did mind this. It made her skin creep, it made her shake all over. It was the dark. She dreaded it. She dreaded being left alone in the dark for ever and ever!

Who would find her? Who would rescue her, alone in the dark? No one!

Woodhouse was right, they would not know where to look. The search party, if there was one, would be out in the park, by the river where she played. They would

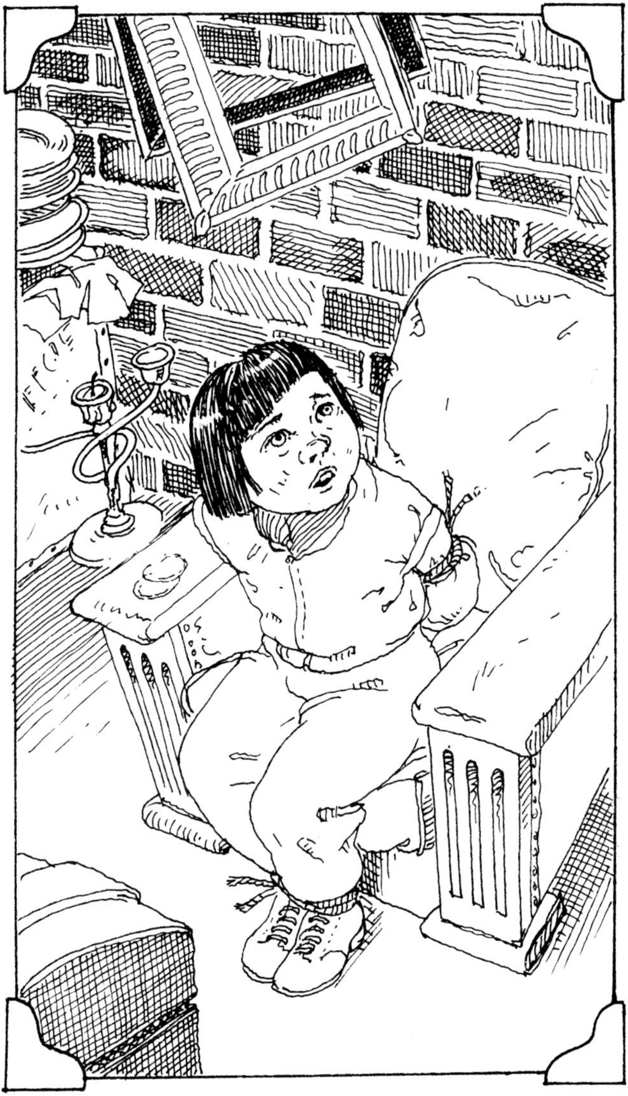

never come to look for her up at Manor House Antiques!

Molly sat amongst old chairs and broken picture frames in the shadows. Her wrists and ankles had already begun to hurt. Time stretched ahead of her like a dark tunnel.

7

"POLICE!"

Fear made her struggle. She had to escape. She knew there were street lights outside this horrible, dark room. She had to get out into the light.

So Molly worked away at the thick blue rope, but it held fast. Then she hit lucky. The rope around her wrists caught on a nail that stuck out of the chair arm. She pulled. The knot began to untie. She felt the rope move, then she eased her hands free.

Molly sighed with relief. She bent and worked fast at the rope round her ankles. At last her legs were free. She rubbed them hard to bring back the feeling in them. Now all she had to do was to get out of this dump! She felt her way along the wall towards a narrow strip of light.

Bump! She stumbled against something big and heavy. It was too dark to see what it was. She felt along the cold, damp wall towards the light.

But there was a noise outside. She froze. She knew that noise! It was the white van again. Molly stood frozen to the spot.

She heard Woodhouse's thin, posh voice. The engine died and two van doors slammed shut. He said, 'Right, Carter, you can leave the rest to me.'

'Sure?' Carter's wheezy voice asked. 'What about the kid?'

'Leave her to me,' Woodhouse said.

Molly heard one pair of footsteps die away, but the others came nearer. A key turned in the lock. Stumbling against things, Molly made for the door.

As Woodhouse opened it and turned on the light, Molly flung herself on the floor. He closed the door. There were faint sounds of cars stopping. Maybe Molly could cry out for help.

But for another second she lay still behind a wooden chest. Woodhouse went across to the empty armchair. He swore and kicked it. The chair crashed against the wall. Woodhouse kicked everything in sight. He turned everything upside-down. Soon he would find her. Molly would have to get up and run for the door.

But Woodhouse spotted her. He charged at her like a mad man.

He grabbed her arm just as a police siren started up. A blue light flashed in the yard. Car doors slammed.

Woodhouse swore again. He threw Molly in front of him like a shield. 'Don't come in!' he shouted. Footsteps in the yard stopped. 'It's not safe in here!' he yelled.

'Take it easy!' a man's voice warned. Everything went quiet.

Woodhouse put his mouth close to Molly's ear. 'Don't say a word!' he whispered. He looked like a caged animal.

Molly nodded. She was scared to death. He held her head in the crook of his arm, close against his chest.

'Who's there? What's the matter out there?' Woodhouse said. He tried to sound normal. 'Let me just clear up some mess in here!'

'Police!' a voice outside said. 'Open the door!'

'Just a moment!' Woodhouse dragged Molly away from the door, back towards the inner door. He opened this one and quickly dragged her down a dark hallway. He was getting away! Molly could not scream with his hand over her mouth.

But she could bite. She bit hard. Woodhouse yelled and let her go, just as another door opened from the front of the house. Lights went on. Woodhouse turned to run.

Then a shape came running towards him. Molly crouched against the wall. The shape charged and knocked the thief down. It sent him crashing down the corridor, sat on him and forced his head back against the cold floor. Molly dared to look up.

'Dad! Dad!' she cried.

Policemen ran in from the storeroom. The hallway was full of dark blue uniforms. Her dad let Woodhouse go. The police hauled him to his feet. Molly ran to her dad.

The lights went on everywhere and she was safe.

8

Photo Proof

Mr Spence kept hold of Molly all the way out into the museum courtyard. 'Here's your mum,' he said.

Molly fell into her mum's arms. Even Paul was there, under the orange street lamp. A policewoman was telling them all what to do. 'We'll sort it all out down at the station,' she said. And the whole family was driven off in a white police car, its blue light flashing.

✧

'Dad, my camera broke!' Molly kept saying. They were trying to ask her what happened. But all she could say was, 'He broke my camera, Dad!'

They were in the police station. Woodhouse was led in, a policeman on either side.

'Ssh!' Mrs Spence said gently. She had one arm around Molly.

The station walls were painted cream. Posters of wanted men and missing persons stared down. A sergeant stood behind the desk. 'What's the story?' he asked.

Woodhouse stood there with his head up, his chin out. 'This is some dreadful mistake!' he said. 'I can explain everything!' He sounded calm, even a bit amused, as if someone had just told him a good joke. The sergeant raised his eyebrows and listened.

Woodhouse brushed himself down and glared at Mr Spence. 'This madman attacked me!' he said.

'He'd got my girl!' Mr Spence jumped up, red and angry.

'Ssh!' Mrs Spence reached out and caught him by the arm.

Molly sat tight. She could not believe what she was hearing.

Woodhouse went calmly on. 'I just went back to my shop to collect a few items. I found this girl hiding in there in the dark. What was I supposed to think? A young thug there in my shop after dark! Hiding in there. I made a grab for her just before

Photo Proof

you lot arrived. Then this mad man attacked me!' Woodhouse looked as if butter would not melt in his mouth.

The sergeant wrote it all down. The policewoman fetched cups of tea. Mrs Spence still had to hold Mr Spence back.

Molly could not keep quiet any longer. 'That's not true!' she stood up and shouted. 'He locked me up! He chased me on to the moor after I'd taken a picture. He broke my camera and he took me back. He locked me up because of the statues'

'Statues?' the sergeant said, sounding interested.

'The church statues. They were in the back of the van!' Molly said.

The sergeant looked at one of his men. 'Any church statues in the back of the van?' he asked.

The policeman shook his head. Woodhouse smiled and nodded.

'But I've got a picture of him and Carter with the statues!' Molly began. Then she stopped. Of course, that film was ruined. It lay in the mud at Mirton Rock, along with her precious camera. Woodhouse had even destroyed her first picture of him coming out of the church! She fell silent.

41

'The girl's as mad as her father!' Woodhouse said smoothly. 'She's made all this up.' He looked down at Molly. 'In fact, I'd like to know what she was doing round the back of my shop in the first place!'

The sergeant frowned. 'Are you saying you want to press charges?' he asked.

'Of course. The girl's a thief. Anyone can see that!'

Nothing would stop Mr Spence now. He stood up and yelled, 'Now just you look here!'

A policeman sat him down again.

Mrs Spence sat shaking her head.

Paul was the one who broke the silence. 'This is the man in the park,' he said, pointing at Woodhouse. 'This is the man who chased Molly!'

Everyone stared at Paul.

Paul stared back. 'He did! I'd know him anywhere!'

'Rubbish!' Woodhouse said. He had lost the smile from his face though. 'He's just lying to help his sister. Well, he would, wouldn't he?'

The sergeant gave him a blank look.

'We can prove it!' Molly's dad said. This time her mum did not say 'Ssh!' Mr Spence

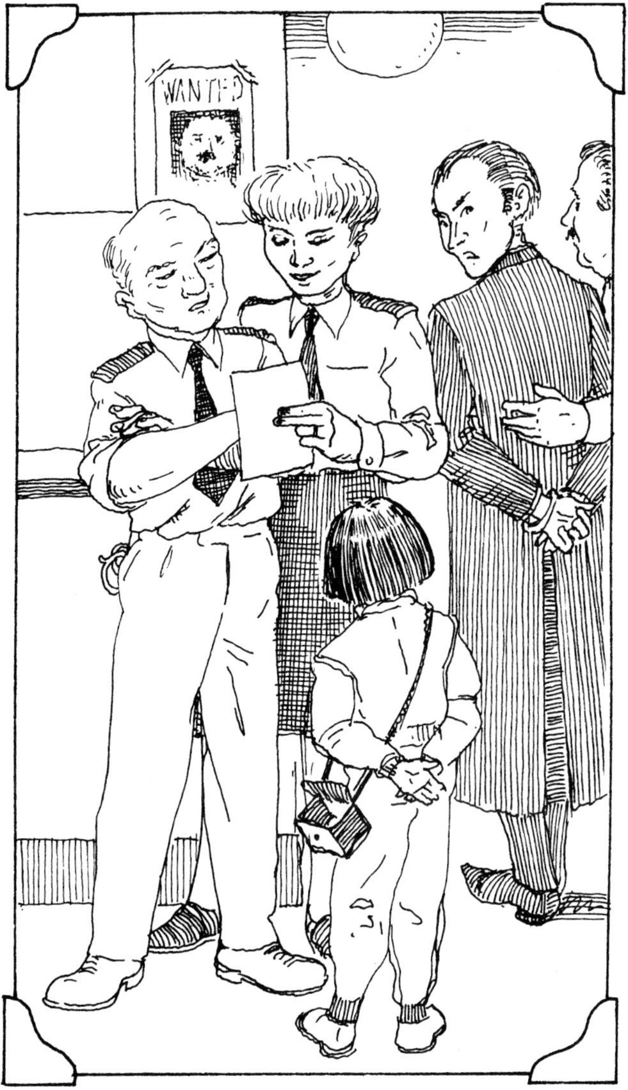
WANTED

stood up and took Molly's hand. 'Come on, Moll, you took this, so you can show him. I made a second print of that church picture. Go on, you show the sergeant!' He gave the photo to Molly.

There was the arched door. There was the face of the thief in the dark coat and grey scarf. There was the bag full of statues. Clear as daylight, Woodhouse stared out from the photo.

Molly handed it across the desk to the sergeant. 'I took it with my new camera,' she explained. 'It was before he chased me and Susie Martin through the park. Paul and Dean tripped him up!'

The sergeant looked at the photo. He looked at Woodhouse, who was white as a sheet. 'Take him down to the cells!' he said.

9

Dream Ending

They marched him out. He went without looking back. He did not say another word.

Molly felt a dark cloud lift from the room. She smiled at her dad.

'You were right,' the sergeant said to Mr Spence. 'Good thinking.'

'Well, Paul brought me Molly's note and the new film,' Mr Spence explained. He was smiling back at her. Her mum was holding her hand. Molly listened to the full story. 'So I printed it quick, like she told me in the note. And I saw the name on the side of the van. Manor House Antiques. Molly said it was a "clue" of some sort.'

'But by then she'd gone missing,' Mrs Spence said. 'I was worried sick. It was tea-time and there was no sign of her. So I rang Keith at his house. We guessed Molly was in trouble. And we guessed it was something to do with church statues and Manor House Antiques!'

'So you came straight to us,' the sergeant finished off. 'You did right.' He turned to Molly. 'And you did a great job,' he told her.

Molly beamed. She turned to each of her family and said, 'Thanks, Mum, thanks, Dad, thanks, Paul!' Paul went red. 'Can we go home now?' Molly asked.

The sergeant nodded. 'We'll charge Woodhouse and the man who was working with him.'

'What with?' Mr Spence asked.

'Burglary and kidnap for a start. Don't worry, we've got plenty of proof.' He waved the photo at them. 'Thanks to you. We'll be in touch.' He smiled and ordered a lift home for all of them. Then he called Molly back. 'You say Woodhouse broke your camera?' he asked.

Molly nodded. The thought of her poor camera nearly made her cry.

The sergeant made a note. 'Well, we can get the cost of the camera back for you if you like. Then you can ask your dad to buy you a brand-new one!'

Molly's eyes shone. 'Can you?'

He smiled and nodded. 'Sure we can.

Dream Ending

It's the least we can do!'

'Thank you,' Molly said. This was ending like a dream. Her mum led her out of the station and the police car took them home. Her dad came in the house with them. Her mum said goodbye to the policeman and closed the front door. Paul made tea without being asked.

They sat round the table drinking tea. 'Will I really get a new camera?' Molly wanted to know.

Mrs Spence put her hand down flat on the table. 'Now listen,' she said. 'If Molly gets another camera I want you all to promise something!'

'What?' Molly said. She was thinking of all the clues she could snap with her new camera.

'I want you to promise me, Molly, that you won't go chasing any more robbers!' Mrs Spence said, as if she could mindread.

'Oh, Mum!' Molly cried.

Mr Spence laughed. 'No, I agree with your mum, Moll,' he said. 'No more clues. Just nice family snapshots from now on!'

For a second Molly sulked. But she didn't really mind. She looked round the table and cheered up. 'I'll start with you then, Paul. You can pose for your photo when I get my new camera!'

'Not likely!' Paul yelped. He shot upstairs.

Molly grinned.

'You'll never put Molly off cameras!' her dad said.

'Never!' Molly agreed.

Some kids like snooker. Some kids like TV. But Molly still liked cameras!